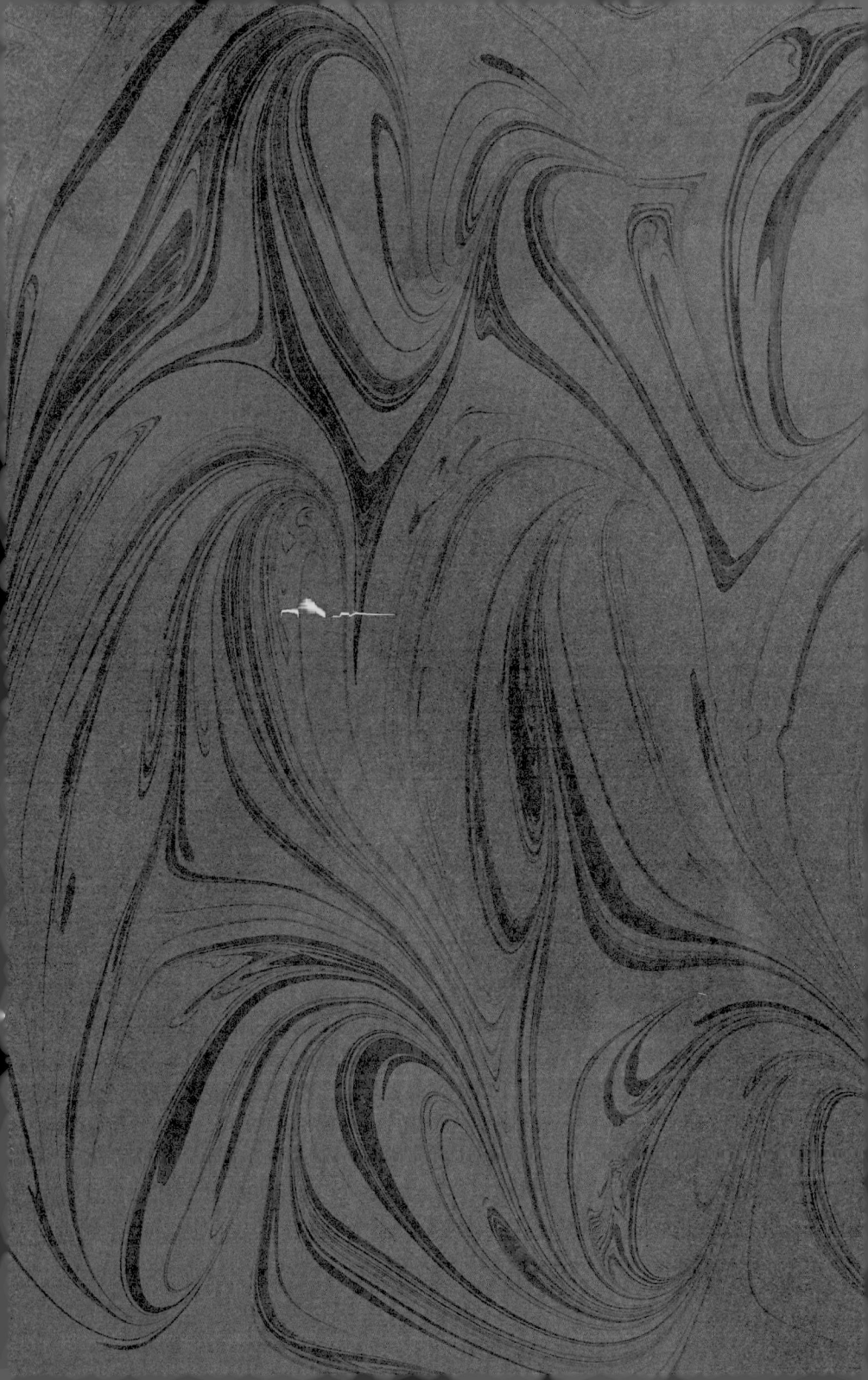

See what great love the Father has lavished on us, that we should be called children of God! And that is what we are!

1 JOHN 3:1 (NIV)

A Father to the Fatherless

AUTHORED BY CARRIE CHRISTOPHER

ILLUSTRATED BY LYNNE HUDSON

*This Book is Lovingly Published By
Lionheart Ministry*

Gospel-Planted Hope

Rejoicing in the Resurrection of Christ

From glory to glory

We proclaim Christ's
ever-infusing love story

The love of the Father sent
down to this earth in love

Displaying His promises, His heroic
attempts to rescue us from above

Perfection was His as He
died in a display of power

His enemies thought His rejection
was the end of His hour

Death had no sting and this
was not the turbulent end

For our Father had a valiant plan,
His Son to sacrificially send

Tears stained the land,
as it was torn apart

Death looked preeminent,

But redeeming mercy was
paving a way for a new start

The dead were raised after
He gave His final breath

It was victory that was seeded
through His willing death

The love of the Father cascaded
through the air of sorrow

Buried were the sins that
Jesus decided to borrow

He carried them,
enveloped in grace,
and tucked under
the earth's core

It was for me and for you
He lovingly fought for

He rose in luminous
soul-awakening glory

Resurrected to rewrite
the fall of man's story

Christ our King would not stay
hidden beneath death's dirt

Triumph was His as He rescued His
Father's children that were hurt

All of us broken, bruised, lost and torn

Can receive His humble sacrifice and
no longer mourn

His peace has been written in
the clouds, His display of power
infused in the soil

Your good works do not make you loyal

It's all about His grace,
His love on display

His gushing gallant grace
that will forever dismay

Father to the Fatherless

A Father to the Fatherless

He was always there
    when there was no one to guide and care

When the aching stirred deep in your heart
    trying to thwart God's plan for you from the start

He was there to graciously hold your hand
    to give you courage so you could stand

He bowed down low to look you in the eyes
    even when you held in your deepest cry

Your heart wept in loneliness, leading you to fear
    wondering why your earthly father was never near

He was building in you a call that would reach the lost
    one full of care and compassion and all it would cost

One that would be marked by your heavenly Father
    one that would never ever make you feel like you were a bother

You're the very child our God is chasing
    no matter the pain and trials you are facing

God's love and light come when everyone else fails
    and even when your earthly father carelessly bails

You are wholly and extravagantly loved
    even when the sin of others has rudely shoved

Drink deeply and taste His great wells of love
    sent from the power of His Holy Spirit dove

You will be heroically set free
>   by His holy blood which sought for thee

This trial will only last for a short season
>   Jesus will teach you His sovereign reason

Cling to Him, who will never let us down
>   even when every other person has made your tender heart frown

He will redeem all that has caused pain
>   and wipe away all the unjustified, spewed shame

God is for you and never apart
>   your heavenly Father, He will never dart

He is truly good, loving and kind
>   all the enemy's schemes, He will valiantly bind

His love so rich and pure
>   all His comfort and security is sure

Find Him in the darkness and in the light
>   let His Holy Spirit heal you and take flight

The hour has come where you will see
>   how much your heavenly Father has loved thee

The moment has come where you will hear
>   there is no longer any strongholds of trauma or fear

You are safe in His powerful arms
>   no longer afflicted by pursuing harm

Close your eyes and place your arms out wide
>   God will remove the lies of abandonment from your inside

*He was always there
when there was no one
to guide and care*

*When the aching stirred
deep in your heart trying
to thwart God's plan for
you from the start*

*He was there to graciously
hold your hand to give you
courage so you could stand*

I write to you, dear children, because you know the Father. I write to you, fathers, because you know him who is from the beginning. I write to you, young men, because you are strong, and the word of God lives in you, and you have overcome the evil one.

1 JOHN 2:14 (NIV)

"Where are you?"
bellows the Lord.

These were our Father's words in Genesis, the reflective care of His intimate heart of cultivation and teaching towards His children. "Where have you run off to? Where have you gone?" These are the trails and the tears of the sovereign, knowing God. He stands at the gates of heaven, proposing a question aimed to teach and gather the hearts of the lost, lonely, fatherless and afflicted. Adam and Eve's first movement of rebellion and sin molded and created the genesis of humanity. The genesis of a generational lineage of sin became our own, riddled with Satan's lies that took the stage in the biblical reflection of His word. We can reflect and ponder our own depravity in sin, paralyzed by shameful hiding and deep waves of regret, ultimately regressing our relationship with Him.

Thank God, our Father and our Maker didn't leave us there. He did not abandon us then, nor will He now. Even if you've been forsaken by earthly fathers, mothers, brothers and sisters. Our God is eternally and forever in love with us as He fought for us by giving the life of His very own Son—the most costly gift He could give, to win us back from the war of Satan. Redemption fills our broken, earthly gardens and longings with an all-pursuing love. A good Father doesn't just let His sinning children run away in sin, shame and hiding. A good, gracious Father creates a redemptive plan that embodies, cares, protects and preserves for the longevity and the generational inheritance of His children, His loved lineage.

You see, we all stem from the Father of lights. If you were created and are living and breathing, then you've been given life by Father God, and He is waiting for you, desiring to care for your every need and commune with you in relationship. The lying, whispering father of lies, the serpent of evil darkness, wants to ensnare the Father's children. You have a choice to make. Whom shall you serve and listen to? Satan the father of lies, or God Almighty, our Creator God? You see, the serpent was disowned by God. He was once an angel but now is permanently fallen to disgrace, and commanded and cursed to forevermore crawl on the earth. You've been given a gift to walk on this wonderment of earth. Satan is continuously motivated by jealousy and hatred over humans, over you, because we have the opportunity to be close to God, and he continues to engage the dark perils of hell to wage war against you. But in Genesis we see a picture painted of a good, loving Father who brings an all-pursuing and consuming love. He is calling your name in the Garden. God laid out the following consequences for the curse of the fall—without a redeemer, we would be separated by God forever. So He made a way. Jesus came to conquer our sin, defeat our shame, and restore us to the Father of Heavenly Lights. God is our forever Father, lovingly perfect and redemptive. He has power, as scripture says, to make all things new, even His relationship with you. He did not leave us or forsake us when we fell short into plunging death and the depths of our sins. He is the same genesis God as He is our present God, by sending His son Jesus to us and for us and filling us with Himself by the presence of His Holy Spirit. To all who would answer this call: "Where are you?"

Are you pondering whether God loves you?

God calls, "Where are you?"

Are you questioning whether God is your Father?

God calls, "Where are you?"

Are you running away in fear, rebellion, shame, and disappointment?

Your Father in heaven is proudly unashamed of you, beaming your name, and pursuing you in spite of your rebellious running away.

"Where are you?"

It is not too late, no matter how long you've been hiding beneath fig leaves.

He is not a Father who abandons. He is not an earthly Father.

To those who feel smited and abandoned by God, say yes.

Call back to God just like Adam responded in the sin-stained Garden of fear.

Speak, "Here I am, my Lord."

As Samuel answered, "I am listening, my Lord."

You see, we all stem from the Father of lights. If you were created and are living and breathing, then you've been given life by Father God, and He is waiting for you, desiring to care for your every need and commune with you in relationship.

My Father Is a Protector

My Father would tear down walls to answer my calls

He would part the red sea to demand enemy forces to flee

He would still the raging storms and disperse Satan's swarms

He would lead me through the dark,
displaying His faithful mark

He would remove me from danger,
promising redemption through a manger

My God would swallow up the earth
to protect what His Spirit has birthed

He would leave the ninety-nine to show me His light's shine

He would engulf all my lies and dry up my tear-stained eyes

He would hush and lull me into rest,
seeing me through every war and test

He would declare I am not defeated,
in His heavenly courts I am seated

He would jump over walls of fire,
reassuring me He never sleeps nor tires

He would promise me still, kind peace,
as my strivings and control cease

He would claim me as His own,
bought by His blood on the cross He atones

I need not to question His calming love,
He was sent on a rescue quest from above

My Father will never ever leave me,
He anoints my eyes with the Spirit's revelation to see

He has never let me go,
His word a trail of promises to faithfully show

My Father, my friend,
loving everlasting grace given until the very end

He promised weapons of war,
through His scars He sacrificially bore

He promised rivers of life,
canceling my debt and sin strife

He promise everlasting love,
giving condemnation a bold shove

He promised safety for my soul,
not a life that's spiritually dull

He kissed peace and lent it,
a gift I can receive and a firm place to sit

A grace prevailing, freedom sailing

Hope unending, ever sending

Presence of life

*My Father would tear down
walls to answer my calls*

*He would part the red sea to
demand enemy forces to flee*

*He would still the raging
storms and disperse
Satan's swarms*

*He would lead me through
the dark, displaying His
faithful mark*

The Spirit you received does not make you slaves, so that you live in fear again; rather, the Spirit you received brought about your adoption to sonship. And by him we cry, "Abba, Father."

ROMANS 8:15 (NIV)

Your Father, The King

He is your defender & your internal mender.

The God of great glory, your heavenly Father, desires to charge all of His angels to guard you.

Run into His presence and be kept wholly covered under the tent of His goodness, care and provisional power.

He is the commander of angel armies. He invites the destitute, the broken, the barren, the lost, the seekers, the smited.

He calls each and all forward to become adopted as Sons and Daughters of His Kingdom.

Let Him Father you. He is whispering, His word is encircling, and His heart is inviting you to join His heavenly family.

You are loved and found in Him.

NAMED

I call you by name, even when you are afar,
chasing after your idols and sin

"I call you by name for you are mine,"
deems and proclaims the Lord

Sin doesn't get to name you
and shame doesn't get to label you

And Satan doesn't get to curse you

"I named you!" shouts the Lord

You are mine

I've named your purpose

I've named your sins on the cross of my Son

I've named your family

I've named your lineage

In the power of my Son's name lays my claim

You have been named under grace,
welcomed to hear the hearty measures of my love in this place

Your name is a legacy, a banner of power

Would you return back to me so I can transform you in this hour?

You've been named, so why do you run
from your sin like that of Moses, my son?

Don't you know the rich blessings that await
your surrendered obedience, my precious one?

Fret not your sorrows nor give way to your transgressions and pain

I am the Lord God almighty who prospers this land

But now, this is what the Lord says—he who created you, Jacob, he who formed you, Israel: "Do not fear, for I have redeemed you; I have summoned you by name; you are mine.

ISAIAH 43:1 (NIV)

The Battle Is Not Ours

Haven't you ever wondered?
Haven't you ever heard?
What is all our suffering for?
Is it pointless or pointed?
Needless or crucial?
Is God sovereign or are we left to determine our own destinies?

Sometimes the paralysis of thinking can punch you in the gut, causing you to rationalize everything to the pointed effort of perfection. To have everything figured out, neat and tidy, answered and known.

But what if a world of wonder awaits in faith? What if the circuitry of challenge is channeled into a horizon of hope in every difficult, weighty circumstance? What if we can wrap our hearts around the goodness of God, our Father's heart, and the eternal? How can it be both and? God is good all the time in spite of life's prevailing difficulties. He is a grace-filled Father always, drawing us near through the hard roads of calamities into the sovereignty of His comfort, over and over and over again. But you see, that's not the end. If we are eternally minded, then everything has an eternal consequence! What we bind here on earth is bound in heaven. What is created in this fragmented reality of earth's time with Jesus is intended to release us from demonic strongholds of the present darkness here on earth and catapult us into the horizon of heaven!

We don't wrestle against flesh and blood. We wrestle to bring salvations here on earth, bringing a multitude of children back to the Father's heart and hand in restoration. We wrestle with our flesh to be unraveled, so our souls can taste death's sting, and so we can finally follow Christ with our whole hearts and minds, looking into His heavenly gaze with a multitude in tow.

Yes, that's right, leaders, we march forward with armies behind us. One so radically on fire with the Lord's truth that we can pummel our enemies with just a song. One so emboldened, like the Lion of Judah, that the laughing hyenas of Satan can

Father to the Fatherless

be doomed to the day of destruction. There is a time coming, army of the Lord, where there will be no more suffering, but in the meantime would you lay it all down, so you can serve your Master? The merciful Master Christ Jesus, the Messiah of righteousness, the crowned King, the Lord above every other Lord. May you walk in triumph, not letting your suffering get another say in the purpose of it. And may you allow the Holy Spirit to tend to and cultivate the word of God richly into your weary hearts. As it is written, "In all things God works for the good of those who love him, who have been called according to his purpose," Romans 8:28 (NIV). Arm up, lock into His gaze and keep on going.

But what if a world of wonder awaits in faith? What if the circuitry of challenge is channeled into a horizon of hope in every difficult, weighty circumstance? What if we can wrap our hearts around the goodness of God, our Father's heart, and the eternal.

My Rescue

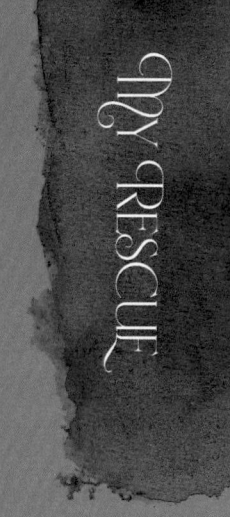

Bend low

Pick me up when I don't know where to go

Show me the paths of Your heavenly love to discover and know

Sweep me up prior to danger's strike

Revive my drought with Your eyes gazing alike

Tune my ears when I've rebelliously shut You out

Give me Your heart to hear Your war cry shout

Diminish within me the fretful ways of operating on my own

Dawn light upon my mind with Your understanding shown

Give me Your heavenly eyes of insight to see what holds me down

Show me Your kingdom blessing inheritance, Your perfect wisdom crown

Teach me to number my days, gaining Your knowledge from afar

Help me to hear You, Heavenly Father,
be to me David's lineage, bright, beaming, promised star

Light in the darkness, illuminating my sin-stained face

Explosive wonder, the expanding, infinite wonders of great grace

Fill me, Father, with embellishments of Your kingdom riches

Rescue me from the places of my lost sin-filled ditches

Forgiveness in Your courts lives on forever

By Your will You've disarmed sin's grip and tether

You will be to me my perfect Heavenly Father, patient and kind

You will only show grace through the cross, a heavenly treasure to find

Holding me, placed upon your heart, while I weep and wail

Giving me courageous strength to overcome and prevail

You are the Father of riches, great and awesome in deeds

Planting in Your children imperishable, holy wonderment seeds

My Abba Father, my only living, loving hope

Perfect in righteousness, my way out of darkness and sin's faltering slope

Bend low

*Pick me up when I don't
know where to go*

*Show me the paths of
Your heavenly love to
discover and know*

*Sweep me up prior
to danger's strike*

*Revive my drought with
Your eyes gazing alike*

And do not call anyone on earth 'father,' for you have one Father, and he is in heaven.

MATTHEW 23:9 (NIV)

To the Wounded Lamb,

Your Father, your Maker has seen all of your tears and how much this life has cost you—the hours and days spent seemingly wasted on the agonizing efforts of emotions and the inner turmoil of your distressed heart. You have lived far from the Father's healing hand, because you've been afraid and ashamed to come close. The enemy of orphanhood has intimidated you through using literal earthly fatherlessness to paralyze you and be your distress. But the Lord shouts no more! No longer will you be welcome to stay on the outside of His Kingdom's riches and the divine courts of His care. Come in, come inside! You don't have to live in an unworthy mentality any longer! You are called sons and daughters of the most high God! You have a calling and you have a place! You no longer need to wander in disgrace!

Grace provides what this world cannot. His compassion can heal every orphan wound! He can sound the trumpet of victory over the bitter walls of Jericho, over the moments of evil you have faced. You've been rescued. You've been redeemed. No longer stay distant. Disgrace and rejection have to tremble at the King's feet. You were made for more and you were destined for this moment. His deliverance has taken so long because there are many more wounded and they need rescue! Would you say yes to be rescued and then go and get the others? Welcome them home, bring them into the flock and protect their lives from wolves in sheep's clothing, wolves that are hidden behind evil wools of temptations. Remove the wool from the baby sheep's eyes. And let them see the Father as a Shepherd, a redeemer and a friend! The Shepherd is pouring holy oil over you right now to heal your wounds.

My Abba

Through the wind

I heard a whisper

It was my Abba Father calling me deeper and wider
into the presence of His all-encompassing, abiding love

I have had tastes of His love before, but never this deep

The love of His breathing miracles, His heart beating in synchronized efforts
with the Son and Spirit, all drumming to the Kingdom's wavelength

Come forward, all you who stand far away

You don't have to look any further

I am your Father here to stay

If you return then I will heal your aching heart without delay

But if you stay there you will forever remain astray

I am coming for the least of these, the broken and the bruised

The ones who are beat down, will be my greatest revival fuse

Light the way for my rich glory to reign down

God your Father gives you not a cold shoulder
but a hearty welcoming crown

"I've been waiting," declares the Father to the remaining flock

Whoever would answer to my pursuing, all-knowing Kingdom knock

Let me in, let me in, before it is too late

I've got gifts to lavish upon you, my inheritance is your fate

Kingdom come, here on earth as it is in heaven

Declaring the remnant, cleansing and cleaning out the leaven

I am breathing hope and my heart is beating a welcoming drum

Declaring your identity and inheritance, I am where you are from

Know me and let me in to heal

I will forever put my love upon you, my Spirit I will reveal

I will boldly carry your ever-flowing sorrows

And hold your heart and hand until heaven's tomorrow

I am the great I am

Calling you to the fold as my precious lamb

*Come forward, all you
who stand far away*

*You don't have to look
any further*

*I am your Father
here to stay*

*If you return then I will
heal your aching heart
without delay*

When Jesus spoke again to the people, he said, "I am the light of the world. Whoever follows me will never walk in darkness, but will have the light of life."

JOHN 8:12 (NIV)

All Things Speak of His Glory

The swaying of the switchgrass by the touch of the breeze and the enchanting canticles of the birds sing and speak of His glory.

Even the creatures created by the Master can't help but worship. Worship becomes my way to the Father, most often a transition between my wrestling to the surrendered return of my praise and pursuit of His heart. A pathway to the immersing presence of His promising power.

I am protected, provided for, and wholly soaring under His cultivated compassionate care. Retreating with our Father never gets old or lonesome. To just be.

Come as you are and become His clay. It is here you can be transformed into hopeful, become patient in the waiting, want to be molded, shaped and beautified into the impressive stature, steadfast and immovable presence of Christ.

Our Father's heart and hands shape us into the impossible conformity and stature of Christ Jesus, through the sanctifying power of His cross' work within us.

Emmanuel God with Us

Our treasure is found only in Him

It is Him

He stands at the door and knocks

Will you let Him in?

He will usher in the best guest company you've ever experienced

Rich grace

Divine mercy

Inner healing

Perfect, redemptive, sure salvation

Intimate, forever, encountered love

He has not forsaken you

Retreat into His presence and you will experience
the living waters of the excellence of Christ

Return to me, bellows the Lord

Return to me, whispers the Lord

I will cut the wicked cord

Return to me, quakes His glory

I want to redeem your story

Return to me

Let it all go

For it's my billowing love I tenderly show

Return to me

My heart is aching

With many treasures worth taking

Return to me, into my safe hands

I've designed you to glisten and glow like the sands

Return to me in the nick of time

It is the hour of my deliverance's prime

Return to me, rest in my oceans of delight

I will restore you and make everything right

Return to me, my beloved lamb

I am your Father, the great I am

Rich grace

Divine mercy

Inner healing

*Perfect, redemptive,
sure salvation*

*Intimate, forever,
encountered love*

He has not forsaken you

I have swept away your offenses like a cloud, your sins like the morning mist. Return to me, for I have redeemed you."

ISAIAH 44:22 (NIV)

Grace Leads to the Cross

There comes a time, a convergence with a life surrendered to the cross, the cross of Christ. A time to fight chastisement, rejection and orphanhood. A time to see, taste and know the risen Lord. Life and death are at hand and which shall one surrender to? Sin leads to death and grace leads to the cross. An intersection between faith and fear. An option to live or die. To die in Christ is to live. When one sinner repents, angels have triumphant celebrations. Heaven's fields rejoice, songs of deliverance rise in victory, and God's overflowing mercy baptizes with living water, life unending. Instead of catastrophe, there is celebration, instead of anger, there is joy. Instead of fear, there is faith. Instead of bitterness, there is forgiveness. Instead of death, there is grace.

Living out of the love of Jesus isn't all miracles and roses. It is a resilient war. It is a radical laying down of one's life at an altar of new beginnings. It is abhorring what is evil, and no longer participating with evil. It is coming against every wicked lie, abusive word, callused heart, and opposing every flattering eye. Returning to the refuge and the rock of Christ Jesus takes repentance. It takes submission. It takes breaking before the altar in total sacrifice to give up living for oneself, to hearken to the Father's voice and hear His call above it all. It means to return and repent. It isn't a joke, or a silly interpretation. The cross is serious. It is a matter of life and death. Experience the total annihilation of sin and flesh or live in dead, white-washed tombs, as lukewarm hearts all headed for a pathway to hell. Wake up, O sleeper. Hear your Savior call before it's too late, before heaven's doors close and the gates of hell widen. Repent now while you have the breath in your lungs. Wail and weep, oh unrepentant sinners. The time is now to usher in the last of the remnant. The Lord is gathering the last of His sheep. Do not receive the mark of the beast, but instead bear the wounds of Christ's sacrificial love for you. What life do you have left? Only God knows. Fear God and live, all you sinners. Return to me, bellows the Lord. Oh lost sheep, come home.

Our Return

Run to the hills

Into my heart and hands of refuge

Run to the hills

Harboring the embodiment of my presence

Run to the hills

Soaking in the Spirit and the satisfying power of Savior

Run to the hills

Return to my heart with fervency

Run to the hills

No more hiding, my anger is not chiding

Run to the hills

Hear my tender voice, submit to my loving, redemptive, rhythmic heartbeat

Run to the hills

I have longed to be your tender Shepherd of rescue

Run to the hills

Come away into my courts of compassion

Run to the hills

Hear the love behind my voice, my faithfulness calling you from ahead

Submit to me, all you who are faint-hearted and forlorn

My presence will satisfy the barren places and the shamed vices of despair

I am a good God

I am your Father

Enough is enough, the persecution of this world can't have you

God is our refuge and strength, an ever-present help in trouble. Therefore we will not fear, though the earth give way and the mountains fall into the heart of the sea, though its waters roar and foam and the mountains quake with their surging. There is a river whose streams make glad the city of God, the holy place where the Most High dwells.

Psalm 46:1-4 (NIV)

The Cross is the Way of Love

The only way to get to the core of one's heart of sin is through the way of love. As I surrender, the cross represents a vertical line of laying down my life because the Father has drawn me in His lovingkindness. The Father reaches down and a horizon of empathy crosses over my life. What was once surrendered now is crossed with life. This spirit that has been slayed will now be fully brought to life, and fully restored through the way of the crucifixion crossing over through the retaliating love of His resurrection! The Prince of Peace kisses my agony with redeeming hope. Every grace-filled proposition is blessed by His intersecting love.

I cannot win many to the cross of resurrection through hatred or anger or from the pointing of an accusatory finger, but rather through open arms resembling the warm embrace of our Father's love. Come one, come all to the redemptive cross. It is this very place of deep, internal comfort that the Lord can release and free you in. It is an invitation into a land of grace, as our King in heaven dresses you with a garment of peace, gives you a harrowing signet ring beaming with His radical love for you, and gives you a cup of forgiveness. Our God, our Father, our King has prepared the most glorious displays of His splendor. His valiant preparations await in His care of redemption! His peace promises you heavenly gain! His glory ignites your very life with the refuge of the cross. His totality and finished work on the cross births in you a newness that births hope into your life and the lives of others! Jesus will never fail you, He will only push you into the realms of forgiveness.

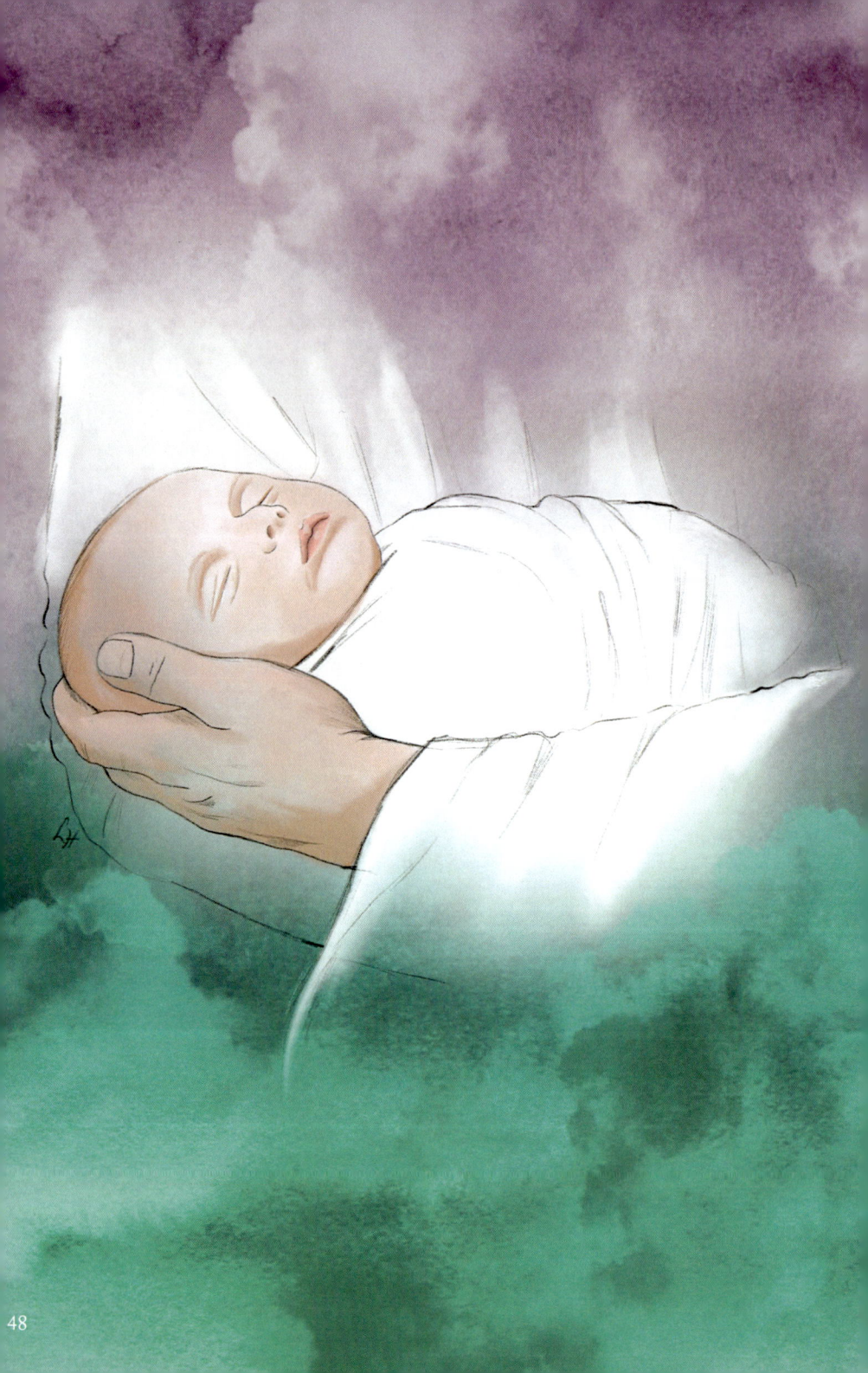

Held in His Arms

I want to sleep in Your arms

Like a baby with synchronized thoughts, sweet dreams

Held in peace-filled gestures of trust

Weightless in Your arms

Resting, trusting, my soul satisfied by Your perfect love

Kept in my heavenly Father's tender care

Divinely made and infinitely held

Streams of living water

Flourishing my heart

Sweetly surrendered I breathe in His love song

My generous Father's lullaby of delight,

Protection and provision fill every valley,

Reach every mountain and carry every sorrow

Held in the arms of my Savior

I am nourished, strengthened and wholly loved

...For the LORD comforts his people and will have compassion on his afflicted ones.

ISAIAH 49:13 (NIV)

The Prayer of Our Hearts

Our hearts cry out to the eternal God, the Father to the fatherless. Speak Lord, for Your servant is listening.

Open our ears to hear Your tender voice calling us forward into the light of all-abiding hope. Bring us into the presence of Your heavenly courts where You are our only hope, our only treasure, found nowhere but in the faithful place Abba.

Give us divine, unshakable confidence that You are sure to deliver us in our place of deep need. Be to us the healing haven of security. Let us soak in the rich layers of Your glory and goodness.

Help My Unbelief

My heart and my flesh cry out

I am willing, forgive me for resisting

I will jump, forgive me for delaying

I will trust, forgive me for doubting

I will go, forgive me for fearing

I will tell, forgive me for being silent

I will know, nothing but what You give

I will hear, all that You whisper within

I will praise, from the depths of my ashes to the grandest mountain heights

I will sing, glory after glory of Your feast prepared

I will prosper, in the land of the Lord's good ways

I will grow, through the bitter accompaniment of suffering with You at my right hand

I will be fathered in the most tempestuous of trials, led and fed

I will be healed from life's most grave, hopeless circumstances

I will carry Your heart to the nations to feast upon Your word

I will bask in the rich waters of the rivers of Your love

Praise the LORD from the earth, you great sea creatures and all ocean depths, lightning and hail, snow and clouds, stormy winds that do his bidding, you mountains and all hills, fruit trees and all cedars, wild animals and all cattle, small creatures and flying birds, kings of the earth and all nations, you princes and all rulers on earth, young men and women, old men and children.

PSALM 148:7–12 (NIV)

His Love Is Your Life

You see, the world can take my dignity and can stifle my courtesy and can forget my every work. But His name shall be remembered. He gets the glory for our stories. The crystallized grains of sand are the salt of the earth and my redeeming refuge shall have the last say.

My victory song is a just cause, "It is finished," that encircles His throne with pleading praises. A holy awakening and a roaring hush is echoing the great King of all king's same words. This battle is ending in a war cry etched upon my heart, "It is finished," mobilizing us to live out that freedom of forgiveness to each and to all.

Otherwise, what are we truly living for, if we are not like the One who paid it all? May our weapons of faith produce the love of Jesus for the lost, the least of these people, like me and you. For He took His own life and laid it down for the Father of lights. Because there were so many more to be recognized and redeemed and ultimately received.

The curated plan for our lives is a living, breathing, Christ-testifying, truth telling of His infinite love, His generous grace and His ministering mercy. Let us linger in this love, lean into this love and live out of this love. Let Him lavish you and fill you with the embodiment of His heart. The atonement of your sins has been won.

Hope in the Storm

On the other side of this mess
    is a sea of redemption

So pure, so holy like a steady sea of glass transpiring peace

On the other side of this suffering is surety
    that your Father, your Maker will clothe you with gladness

On the other side of this trail of tears
there will be bold purposes seen

The lame will walk and the blind will see

The powers of eternity are working and weaving His glory in the rescue

On the other side of this field of labor
    there will be reaping.

Steady hands of harvests will pour out rapid displays of His blessings

On the other side of this paralyzing confusion of thunder
    there will be a chariot ready and waiting to bring you to revolutionary
    heights of heaven, pure and vast beyond your understanding

On the other side of this weapon-built war there will be rejoicing
as His ministering mercy meets you in the power of His breath

Intervention will arrive, His hope will heal and His glory will respond,
clearly hearkening His triune-God purposes in all suffering

The blind receive sight, the lame walk, those who have leprosy are cleansed, the deaf hear, the dead are raised, and the good news is proclaimed to the poor.

Matthew 11:5 (NIV)

Our Refuge in the Storm

Retreat and take refuge in your Father, your eternal heavenly maker, while in the storm. There is an umbrella of grace extended to you who is warring spiritually against the wind and the waves.

Fret not, fear not, for your Lord is with you. He will hush you into His presence and lull you in the billowing winds of His love. Listen to His reassuring calming voice of security.

This world can paralyze us with danger but rest assured, our Father, our friend will be our helper. Storm surges are but for a fleeting moment, the calm of the sea shall surrender to His will and way.

Trust in the Father, cling to the Son, and listen to the omnipotent voice of the Holy Spirit.

My Faithful Father

You have a faithful Father singing over you
and a father of lies whispering demise

Hear your Father's voice

The only freedom choice

Your Father is calling

Don't let fear keep you stalling

Come to Him in moments of surrender

Receive His promise to never ever plunder

The Father of your faith is drawing you near

Open your heart to eagerly hear

I've loved you, I've drawn you through my kindness

I've chosen to give you new life and heal your spiritual blindness

I'm here, shouts your Abba, the ancient Maker of old

I'm your Good Shepherd, inviting you into my heavenly sheep's fold

It just takes one yes, and a surrender of your pain

I'm here to hold you and equip the seemingly slain

Call upon my name of heavenly lights

I've come to forgive you, and I've put my life on the line as the fight

I've promised you eternal life

To end sin's sufferings and strife

To give you a calling,

Crowning you with gifts enthralling

I've chosen you to shine as my bright, beaming jewels

I'm going to heal you and equip you with my Kingdom's tools

A fortitude of faith is what I'm pleased to provide

Open up your heart to receive what I'm going to pour on the inside

Love upon love

Grace upon grace

My love surpassing all your sins and taking its place

Hear your Father's voice

The only freedom choice

Your Father is calling

*Don't let fear
keep you stalling*

*Come to Him in
moments of surrender*

*Receive His promise
to never ever plunder*

*But you, God, see the
trouble of the afflicted;
you consider their grief
and take it in hand. The
victims commit themselves
to you; you are the helper
of the fatherless.*

PSALM 10:14 (NIV)

A Prayer For Our Revival

Holy Spirit, let our hearts and our homes be a haven, a haven for heaven's work in us and through us.

May the heart of God position our families and the generations thereafter to hear from You and respond with zeal.

Have Your way within us, gracious Father! Do not delay in resurrecting our dead flesh into spiritual manna for the lost and least of these.

Have mercy on us and equip us to know the heights and depths of Your unrelenting love. You are the Father of our faith, the eternal, beaming, glowing, seeking and reaching light from heaven's abode.

Bring heaven down to earth, come and rescue us from our desperate shadows of sin's plight. We are burning for you, Father of our Faith.

His Revelation Light

The revelation light of my glory and King

Invites my heart to surrender, to release and to sing

The freedom that the word of God's truth creates

Ministers to my soul with weapons to state

Fear cannot have me, my faith remains sure

The Lord, my Father, remains holy and pure

His ways inside of me perplex me with great wonder

His word awakening me like provoking thunder

Agitating my sin, bringing me to His grace-filled courts

Discovering what sin holds me down and what Satan attempts to thwart

My Father is a triumpher, a Maker, the King of all kings

He will rescue His children and place on their hands redemption rings

My Father has called me higher

Through the exposed work of Satan the liar

Delivering me from oppositional ashes

Healing my life's inner throbbing thrashes

My soul now saved, soothed and free

Found by my Father, given spiritual eyes to see

Meeting my Maker brings great joy to my soul

Returning me to Abba, deliverance in full

He will stand and shepherd his flock in the strength of the LORD, in the majesty of the name of the LORD his God. And they will live securely, for then his greatness will reach to the ends of the earth.

MICAH 5:4 (NIV)

The Cry of Our Hearts

Hold our hearts today, Father, as we are hurting and yearning for healing. Hold our hands, Father, as we are fearing what is next.

Whisper Your wonderful ways into our inner beings as we wait for deliverance. May your radical wisdom encircle and impart Your glorious ways to us as we search.

Fill every hungry, parched place with profound encounters with Your word and presence. Shepherd, steer your sheep from danger, lead us onward into pastures of praise.

Be our helper, lifting us high and mightily into gates of Your glory. Defend us in the schemes of the enemy, clothing us with splendor and garments of eternal Spirit-filled fruit.

Vindicate us and push us forward in faith, by faith.

REASSURED AS TREASURED

I am like a baby held,

Rocked, lulled and shushed

I am like an infant crying,

Satisfied, soothed and cradled

I am like a child's wanting,

Nourished, strengthened, affirmed

I am like one who has fallen down,

Lifted up, reassured, treasured

I am like the one who has gone the wrong way,

Redirected, guided and encouraged

I am like the one who has given up,

Rebuilt, edified, enriched

My true Heavenly Father is loving, kind, perfect and present

Never leaving me nor forsaking me

Found

Protected

Nourished

Strengthened

Edified

Encouraged

Taught

Bought

Chosen

Whole

Father to the Fatherless

"Truly I tell you, unless you change and become like little children, you will never enter the kingdom of heaven. Therefore, whoever takes the lowly position of this child is the greatest in the kingdom of heaven. And whoever welcomes one such child in my name welcomes me."

Matthew 18:3–5 (NIV)

Surrendering to You

You are God, I am not. I must die to my failing, fleeting, feeble flesh. My control wants to overtake my agreement to complete surrender and trust. My plans want to override the circumstantial regret and gruesome guilt plagues. If I could only surrender to the calamity moment by moment, trusting minute by minute.

Equip us with Holy Spirit action so we can soar on eagle's wings in freedom. Whatever our Father says must be the fabric of our very beings. I acknowledge the things I am powerless to change. And to hear my Father's heart in all situations to prosper me forward requires deep trust and deep surrender.

Let it be according to Your word and Your will. I am but dust—sinning, broken, feeble and in desperate need every moment for the leading of my Father, my Maker, my Eternal. I am a child humbly broken, atoned by Christ's blood. Awe and wonder arises at what the Lord shall do in and through our surrender to our Savior.

As You work within us, functioning, teaching our minds and hearts how to trust, bring us peace, as our surrender brings us Your hope. Bring recompense. Bring justice. Bring holiness. Bring purity. Bring movement, allocation in the heavenlies and authoritative power as a prospering people. Let Your Body be a surrendering Sainthood, relinquishing all plans and all control.

The Great Generous Grace Giver

The wind beneath my sail

The glorious opportunity to prevail

The notion of my heart to be heard

Freed swiftly and radically like a bird

Flying, soaring, through heights of His grace

Knowing where and how to take my heritage place

Prepared, unharmed, protected and free

Held in the arms of my Savior, equipped to see

I'll tell the church and the generations beyond

Of the love of the Father that my heart is so fond

The glory of my risen Lord

The lands of grace that I have toured

His totality of the cross

Redeeming my sins, suffering no eternal loss

Freed, captivated, tried, and taught

No longer oppressed but by Christ's blood I am bought

Sin fleeing, the cross planted, invited by my Father
into the freedom lands of grace

Father to the Fatherless

For it is by grace you have been saved, through faith—and this is not from yourselves, it is the gift of God—not by works, so that no one can boast.

Ephesians 2:8–9 (NIV)

Our Father Loves Us

You are purposed to live in the land of free grace under the shadow of the almighty, all-providing Abba Father. To live under your Father's tender cultivation means He will prune you, water you and feed your soil's nutrients to grow up in the strong stature of praise and worship of your Gardener.

The Lord loves His children, more than we can imagine and fathom. His love is from everlasting to everlasting, always coming after us to chase us down with His goodness. We cannot meet our Father and stay in the unbelieving waters of orphanhood. When we meet our Father we are forever changed and transformed by and through His heart.

The Lord upholds all power by and through His word. The Lord breathed into your lungs a divine purpose to ignite your Kingdom inheritance from death to life, from orphan to His child, from sin and slavery to grace-filled salvation.

FAITH AND TRUTH RISING

Truth is tossing to and fro in my turbulent mind

Unbelief is speaking fear and attempting
to unearth what the Lord has planted

Total sobriety, abstaining from all
that would grant access to the enemy

Victory vices are rising up to take back
the ancestry of the venomous avenger

Promises pounce and ravage what the Lord has
proposed and planted, pruning my soul with power

The word overturns the whispering ways of the estranged one,
and I no longer wallow in them

Truth teaches and triumphs over my incarnate mind,
telling the taskmaster to submit to the Teacher

Abba Father, my soul answers to the
only One who can arrange for hope to fill

My God is able

Fear is now fretting at the sound of faith, and the fingerprints
of God's work coming to fruition leads me to freedom

My soul is known, soothed and secure, surrendered and safe,
all-nourished and strengthened in the arms of my Father

Every good and perfect gift is from above, coming down from the Father of the heavenly lights, who does not change like shifting shadows.

JAMES 1:17 (NIV)

Our Heavenly Protector

Praying for you to be free—freely captivated into the paths of peace provided by His presence. May freedom teach you what Christ paid for you. He won it all and provides for our every need. The Lord your God will never leave you nor forsake you but will be your comforter.

The Holy wind of heaven is refreshing you in weariness and is sustaining you on the battlefield during the long, hard hours of your earthly struggles. Your Father watches over you in love, with plans and prayers over every opportunity to redeem what is broken.

Watch and wait as our heavenly Father invades linear earthly time with His heavenly appointed times and seasons of interventions. He is close to the brokenhearted and the crushed in spirit.

FREE FORGIVENESS

A little room to breathe

Gives space to conceive

A weighty display of His glory

Through the bounty of His provision

His storehouses are bountiful,
overflowing and vast beyond measure

A hope, a light, a sure foundation beneath my feeble feet

Is where my soul can freely take flight

On eagle's wings I fly

Solely dependent and trusting

Carried by His strong winds of bearing grace

I look to the right and He is beside me

And to the left and His Spirit leads me forward

And as I look upward I am bound to encounter the Father's heart

His eyes brimming glossy with tears of delight in His blessing of a child

A proud papa

Not forlorn or scolding

But freely forgiving and abounding in rescuing grace

Singing a triumphant tune with love on His face

This is my Father, my Abba

"Do not store up for yourselves treasures on earth, where moths and vermin destroy, and where thieves break in and steal. But store up for yourselves treasures in heaven, where moths and vermin do not destroy, and where thieves do not break in and steal. For where your treasure is, there your heart will be also."

Matthew 6:19–21 (NIV)

Your Father Adores You

He beams proudly over you. He is not disappointed or ashamed of you. But instead, He is immersed in love for you—a love so deep that this world cannot contain the mighty measurements of the heights and depths.

He sings over you with great passion and delight. He takes pleasure in you and fights with angel armies defending your faith path to His kingdom. He calls you forward with all-encompassing joy.

Do not be afraid but go boldly to the throne of grace. And the grace that God offers will cover each and every sin. Knowing your Father's voice will unlock all the promises of God forevermore.

Heaven's Kisses

Heaven's kisses

As grace abounds

A dance with God is where I'm found

Heaven's kisses

As mercy meets

Filling my body with hope from my head to my feet

Heavens kisses

Love is in the air

God's comforting hush whispers His presence everywhere

Heaven's kisses

Pushing back fear

Holding my every aching, travailing tear

Heaven's kisses

My soul alive

Free from a life of perfectionism and a heart strive

Heaven's kisses

As grace prevails

Grace rains in the depths like a powerful hail

Heaven's kisses

His aroma awakes

Coming back for the lost with a vengeance to take

Heaven's kisses

An hour of alarm

This is our Father's love as we are held in His arms

Heaven's kisses

In peace I will trust

Inhabited by the presence of His power, worship I must

*You have been set free
from sin and have become
slaves to righteousness.*

Romans 6:18 (NIV)

Your Refreshment Is in Him

Awaken to the symphony of His voice. Let His word melt every hardened place of deceitfulness and sin. The fountain of the Father is waiting to pour living water over every parched place.

Fruit is slowly growing in long seasons of waiting. He is a skilled sanctifier, saving our flesh from eternal wrath. He is gesturing you forward into heights of heaven, singing amazing grace as a declaration over your life.

Ask the Father for a gift today and wait with expectancy to encounter His heart.

EXPRESSIVE LOVE

The expressive love of the Father

Reaches every risen molecule,

Every empty cavity,

Circulating the air,

And lavishing every inch in space

His expressive love sings over the barren agony of one's soul,

Wraps up mysteries of prevailing purposes
and plants them upon the hearts of His hungry children

He approaches the lost with direction,
carries strength to the struck down and stricken,

Gives His ear to the cries of His people,

Moves demonic forces aside from the faithful paths and plans of His chosen

He defeats the wicked and burns their
careless actions down to the dust of the earth

He provides safety in the midst of a world of wolves and feeds
the hungry hurting lambs with His overflowing miraculous ways,

Continually filling the earth with the bountiful provision of
His blessing, and providing His fortress of tender love and care

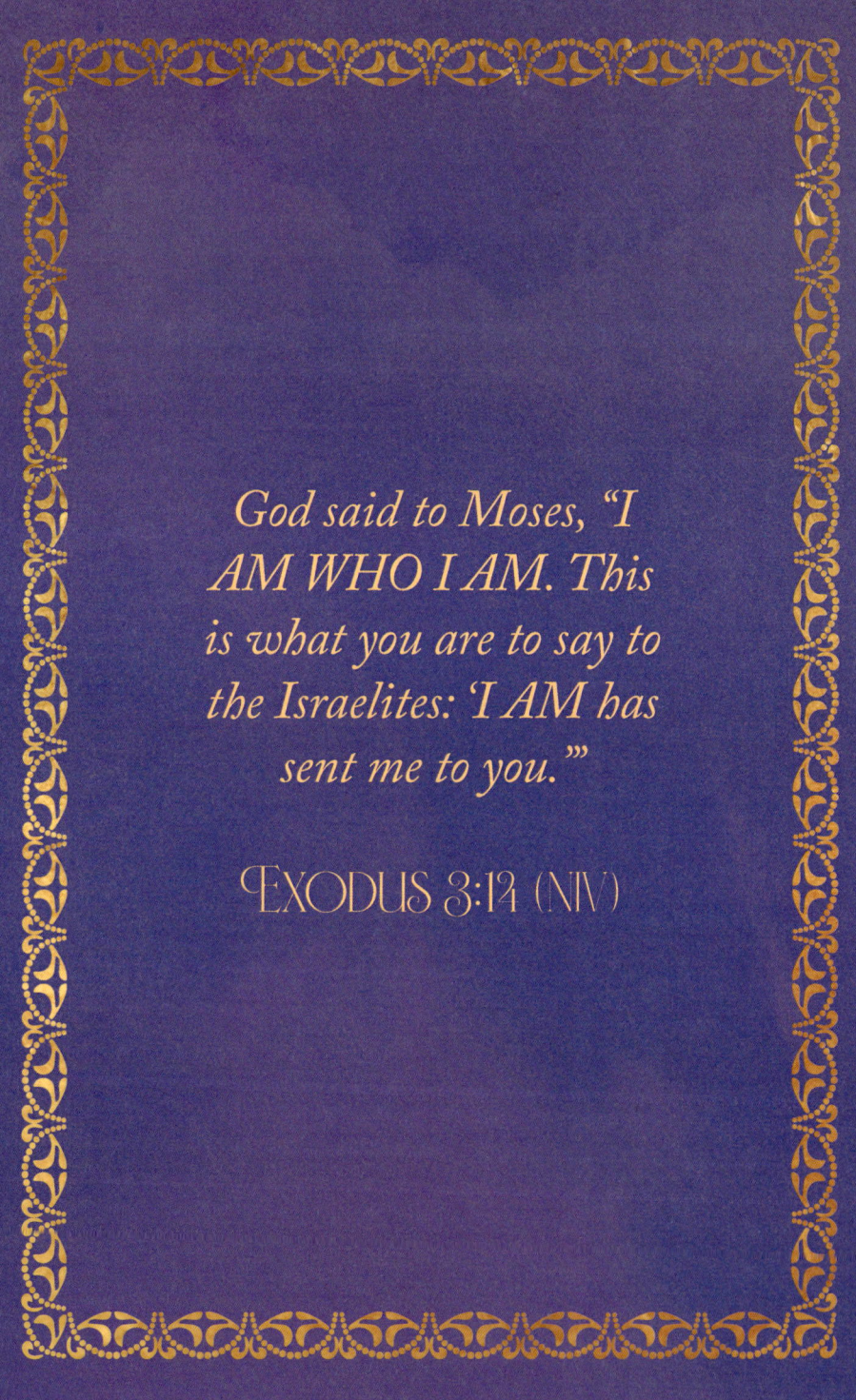

God said to Moses, "I AM WHO I AM. This is what you are to say to the Israelites: 'I AM has sent me to you.'"

EXODUS 3:14 (NIV)

Relationship with Our Father

His love for you was expressed on the cross. The ultimate satisfied longing of redemption on behalf of His Father's heart was provided through redemptive sacrifice.

The way of the Father carries endless banners of meeting mercies, providing peace and giving grace. He provides for us a path of refuge and hiding in the storms of fear.

The Lord listens to the cries of His people and bends a faithful ear to intercede and intervene. He delights in our questions, ponderings and curious bewilderments as we ask for revelation of His mysterious ways.

Interact with the Father today as you call upon His name. He is longing to linger with you, engaging your mind and freeing your heart.

My Destiny Determined

God-sized destinies collide in awe
and wonder with His valiant force

In the former times, the enemy's vicious berating
raged the seas of your heart, storming fear

But behold the Lord is doing something rare and new

Vast and mighty wavelengths of hope
are ministering deeply to your weary heart

Pedals of flowering fruit are growing out of a desert

Victories are booming from the Father's heart unto yours

"Fear not, for I have redeemed you," speaks the Lord

He is calling you by name to come forward,
out of wandering and into your destiny

A destiny road mapped by the Lord's great glory

A Father's hand reaching for His child's trust

Behold He makes all things new

The gifts, treasures and long-awaited prophecies are pointing
you down a path of the pursuing power of Papa the provider

Feast on the fruit of His love

Drink deeply and richly from the Holy Spirit's watering well

Reach high and feel the embrace of His hand leading you to the promised land

Freedom resounds, angels herald, truth tells, lies loosen, Satan sinks, and
fear falls, as Jesus journeys with you to justified junctions of jasper-enriched,
God-sized glories within you and me

Freedom calls and His power speaks, soaring on wings of eagles,
rising high on heights in the heavenlies, soaring free

Once in captivity, you are now unshackled with depths of His
equipping love, undergirding your thirsty soul with deliverance

Dip your toes in the river of life where love lives, where
a lavished labor on the cross bought life and life abundantly

Jeweled junctions are set before your feeble feet,

Now released and equipped to live out your destiny,

To connect your triumph, leaving behind your pain,

To reconcile your losses, bridging the purpose
of your suffering to the very heart of God

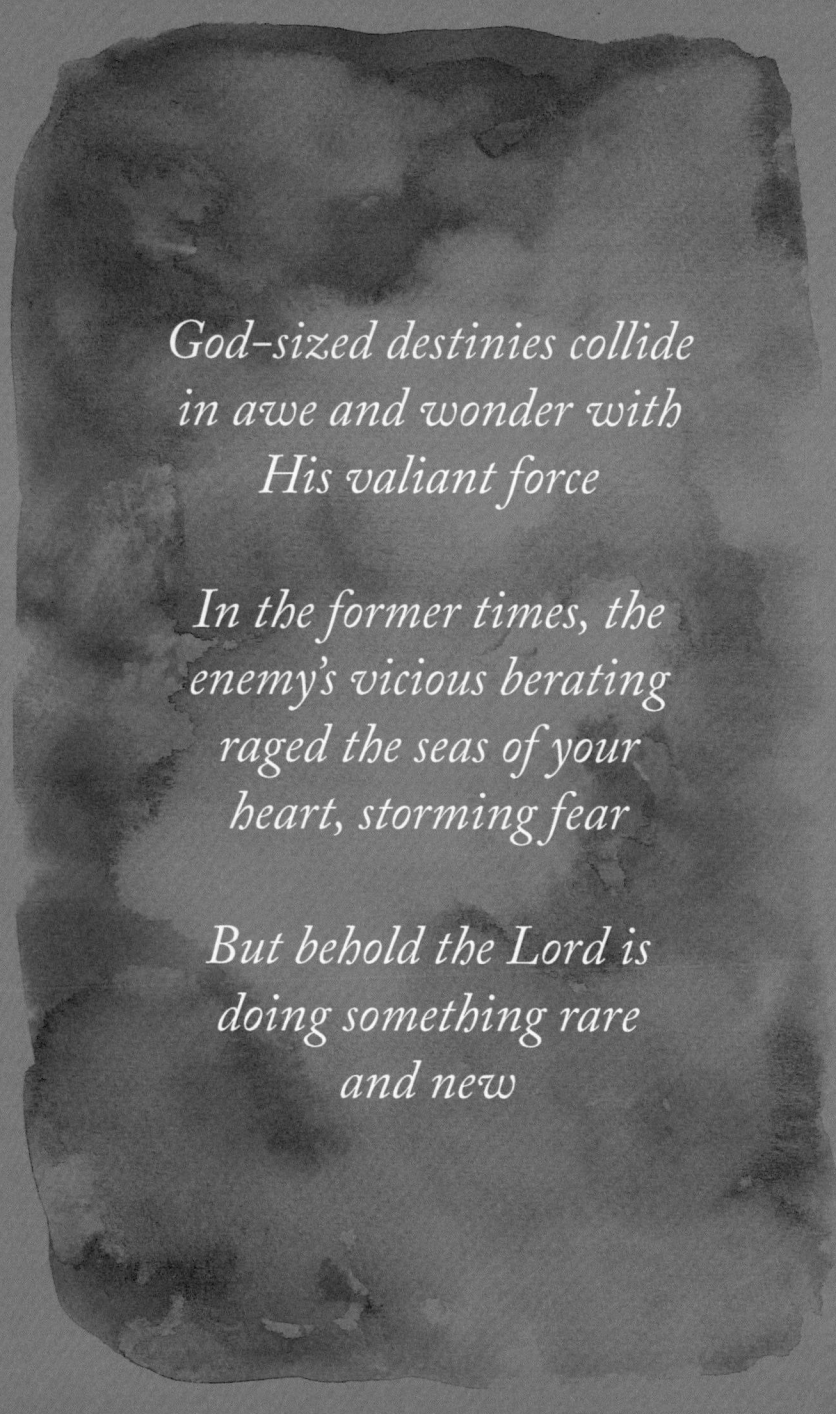

*God-sized destinies collide
in awe and wonder with
His valiant force*

*In the former times, the
enemy's vicious berating
raged the seas of your
heart, storming fear*

*But behold the Lord is
doing something rare
and new*

"I am the true vine, and my Father is the gardener. He cuts off every branch in me that bears no fruit, while every branch that does bear fruit he prunes so that it will be even more fruitful. You are already clean because of the word I have spoken to you. Remain in me, as I also remain in you. No branch can bear fruit by itself; it must remain in the vine. Neither can you bear fruit unless you remain in me."

JOHN 15:1-4 (NIV)

True Rest is Found in Him

I thank our Father as the Holy Spirit's rain pounds my soul with deep deliverances. As deep calls to deep, my pierced heart responds to the tenderness of my Father.

Permeating graces dance in deep jubilance as my soul rejoices in the blood of the Lamb slain for me and slain for you.

As He heaps peace upon peace, upon even the most barren places of my soul, I am drenched in His deep secret hiding places of refuge.

My Father's Heart and Hands

A Father's heart,

A Father's hand

Giving faith to the weak

And the needy to stand

Simply put, God lives and reigns

Pulsating victory through our weary veins

Into our hearts, transforming our minds

Goodness, mercy and His peace are there for you to find

God will not leave you, nor push you away

The presence and generous grace of the Almighty is here to stay

Faithful truth aimed at your anxious heart

Propelling you forward by grace into a new start

A Father's heart,

A Father's hand

Doing immeasurably more than you could ever have planned

Transforming your zeal

Into His Spirit you feel

The breath of His light

Giving you freedom flight through the darkest of nights

Unfathomably so

Does His Spirit willingly go

Into the depths of your being

So you will be kept seeing

His arrayed splendor

His heart so tender

Timely and true

He's coming after you

To bring a display

A wonderful array

Of a Father's heart,

A Father's hand

Grace and mercy so you can reverently stand

A Father's heart,

A Father's hand

Giving faith to the weak

And the needy to stand

Simply put,
God lives and reigns

Pulsating victory through
our weary veins

A father to the fatherless, a defender of widows, is God in his holy dwelling. God sets the lonely in families, he leads out the prisoners with singing; but the rebellious live in a sun-scorched land.

PSALM 68:5-6 (NIV)

His Voice is Your Strength

Deep rivers flow where His deep love grows, as the
cisterns in my soul fill every fretful place that was starved.

From dust my life began, called into His resurrection
plan. An unshakable song of glory is arising with
His tune of grace surprising.

A treasure chest of innumerable wonders is waiting to
be released while hearing my Father's voice thunder.

Open the word of God today and find His voice heard.
May the word stir up an appetite for more.

He is a faithful Father and friend, longing to give
you gifts from the treasure chest of His heart.

REALMS OF FAITH

Deeper, closer, wider still

Take my faith and expand it to the depths of Your holy hill

Take me up to the mountain where I must trust

Losing every fear and hindrance is a must

Boasting that Christ has conquered each and every one of my wars

He's painting a picture of what all my suffering was for

Circular faith, coming closer to the center

A full love, Holy Spirit light as my glorious mentor

Faith fills me, overtaking my every sense

Showing me that His glory and truth are transforming and dense

Full, full, is this wide-open place

A place of adorning, an anointed worship space

Linger in the invitation to be close to our Father

I retreat and bask in His soothing heart

Recharged and set forward as His grace has given me a new start

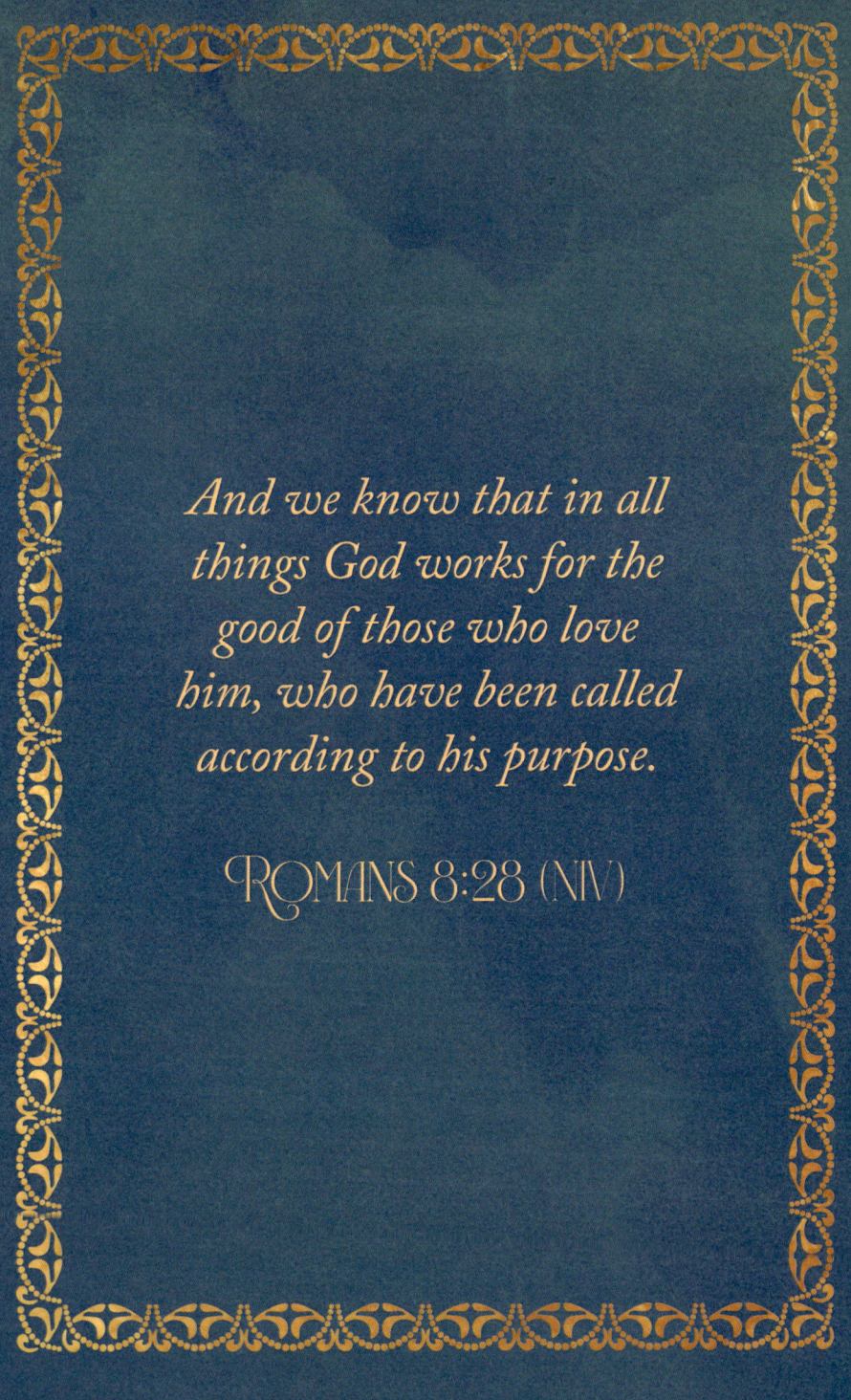

And we know that in all things God works for the good of those who love him, who have been called according to his purpose.

ROMANS 8:28 (NIV)

A Prayer for Transformation

Edify and encourage my inner being with Your triumphant word. I am hungry to hear in the midst of a busy, chaotic, muffled world of wandering.

Bring me into the depths of Your compassions and birth within me what is pleasing and honoring in Your sight.

Curate in me courageous hope in the face of the impossible. Move in the miraculous and set captives free.

Let me be a listening vessel, a son or daughter who lingers in Your love, captivated and transformed.

Surrendering to My Savior

The only thing

Worth dying for is Christ

The only thing worth living for is Christ

The only thing worth surrendering to is Christ

Christ in all, for all, and to each and all

We have empty hearts desiring to be filled

Make way for Christ to enter into your sacred place

A holy spot reserved for your soul to be filled
with His indwelling Spirit

There is no other God but Christ

No other way to the Father,

No other way to inner healing and soul-saving salvation

Christ didn't come for the good, or the perfect,

Or the righteous,

But for the sinner,

The sinner who knows their need for a Savior

A peace-keeping, soul-abiding,

All-encompassing-love place designed to only be filled by our Creator

Once separated,

Now held eternally

Once apart and distraught,

Now perfectly kept and still

Once storm-tossed and afflicted,

Now sheltered and abiding,

Forever hiding in the soul care of the presence of our Almighty

Death has no power, no sting, and no gain

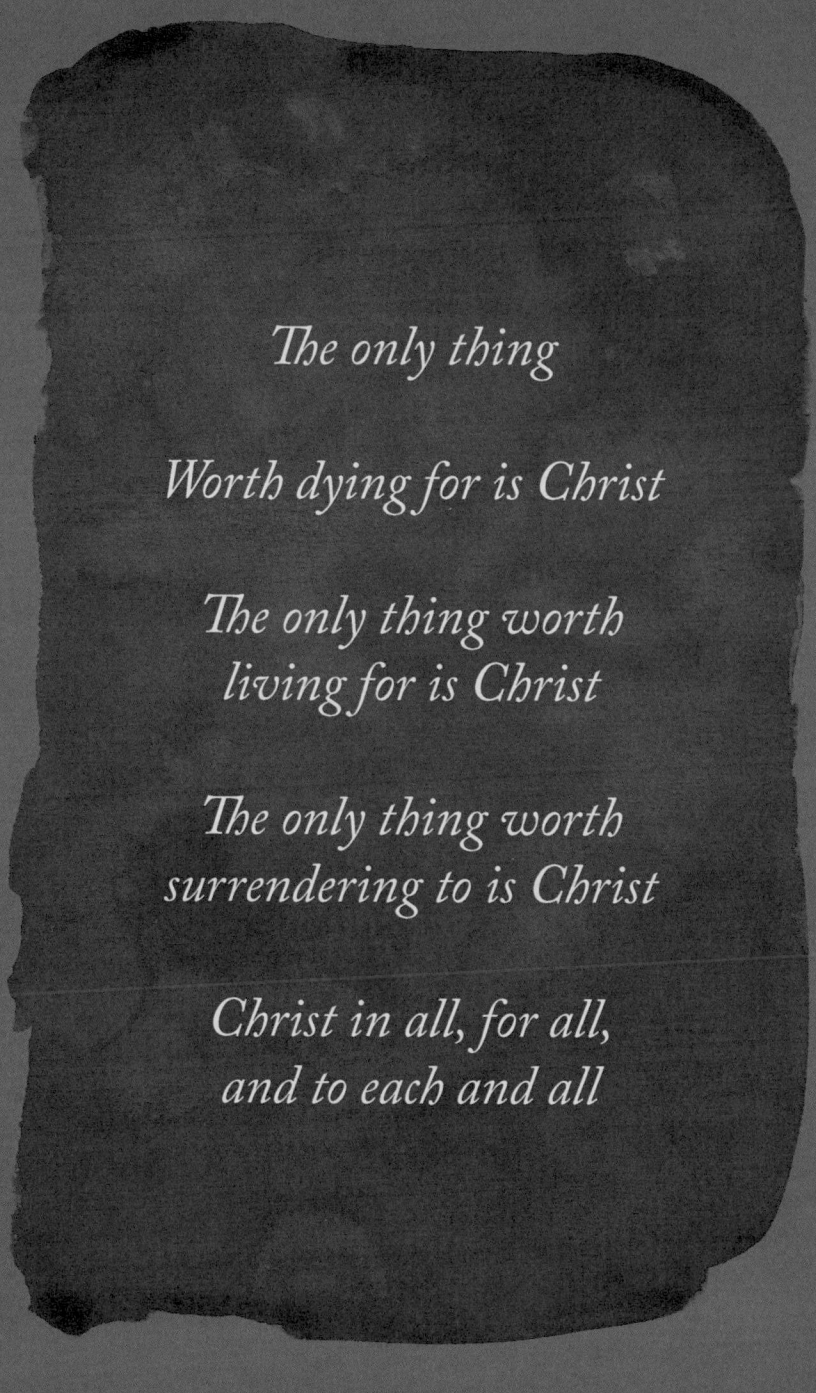

The only thing

Worth dying for is Christ

The only thing worth
living for is Christ

The only thing worth
surrendering to is Christ

Christ in all, for all,
and to each and all

I thank my God every time I remember you. In all my prayers for all of you, I always pray with joy because of your partnership in the gospel from the first day until now, being confident of this, that he who began a good work in you will carry it on to completion until the day of Christ Jesus.

PHILIPPIANS 1:3–6 (NIV)

An Invitation For Your Heart

May the God of all glory fill you with peace
as you believe and trust in Him.

May His truth anoint your mind with the
rich and vast mentality of Christ Jesus.

May surrender be your reaction to the
invitational love that our Father offers.

He is the only way, the truth and the life, and
by Him and through Him we can overcome.

Come empty to be filled.
Come hungry to feast on His word.

Come ready to hear, and come weak
to be strengthened.

Sit at His feet and learn the mysterious
ways of His living revelations.

Flourishing in Victory

On the hem of my Father I ride,

Glory abiding on the inside

Grace filling the temple of my praise,

Rising higher as I release His fragrance in these dark days

From glory I run and through His living water, I am freed

The revival of the risen Lord is picking up speed

Flourishing in victories and rising above,

Flying in triumph with the Holy Spirit's dove

Miracles are releasing as mysteries are revealed

God's mighty ways are no longer concealed

His valor is booming in the wake of His wonders

His voice is triumphing over the enemy as retaliating thunders

The glory of transpiring grace

Overwhelms me with joy on my freedom-deemed face

Glory, glory, glory

Releases the true, eternally saving story

His word written on a prevailing scroll soaring,

Beaming bright beauty of the Lord into nations is touring

Freedom, freedom, freedom is ringing

As the angels' choirs of peace-filled harmonies are singing

Saturated, implanted and brought in a symphony shout

The Lord is coming to free captives from this war-drenched drought

Declaring that He is a Father, a teacher and King,

Planting promises through Christ's covenant, an eternally-given ring

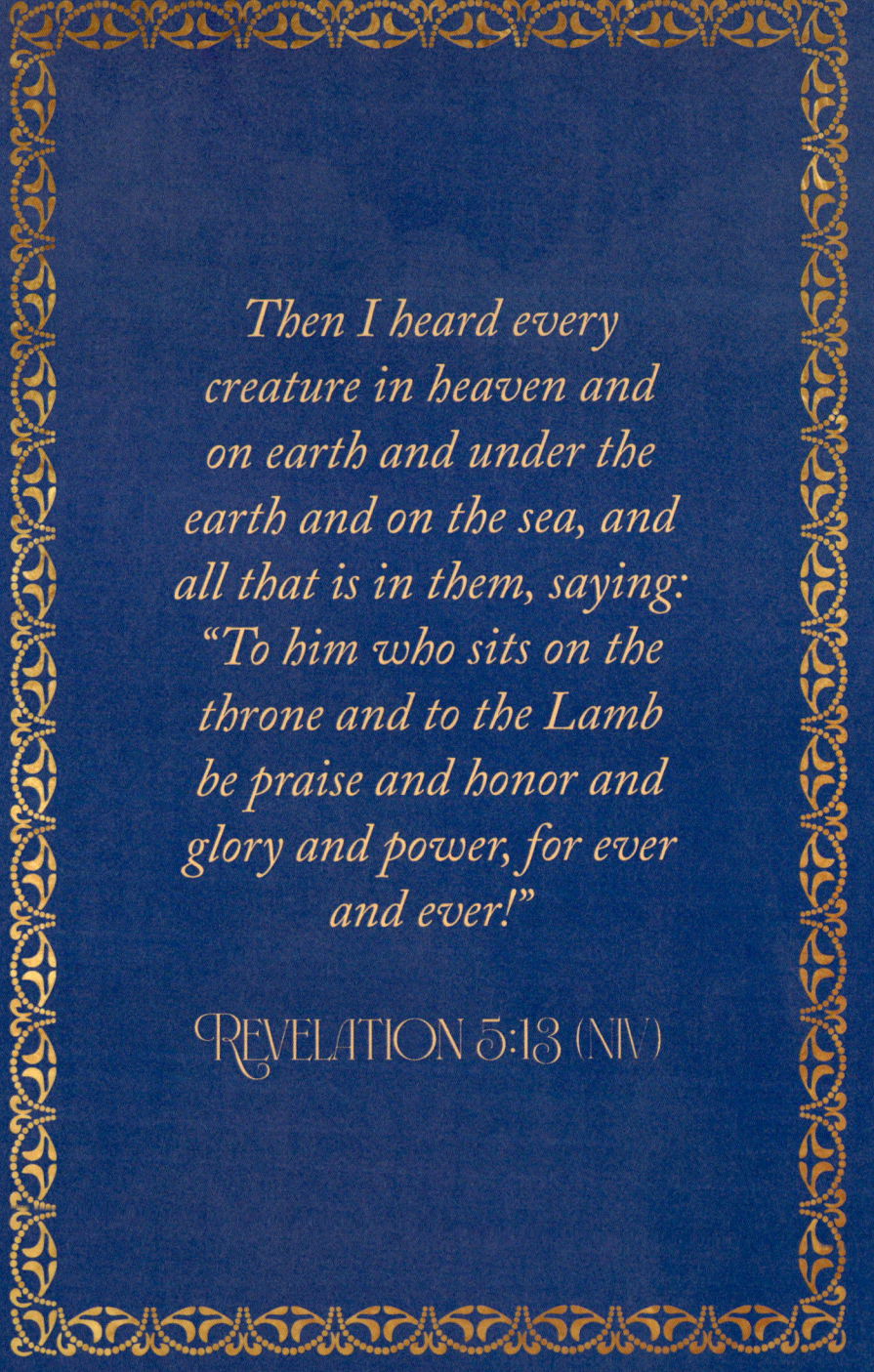

Then I heard every creature in heaven and on earth and under the earth and on the sea, and all that is in them, saying: "To him who sits on the throne and to the Lamb be praise and honor and glory and power, for ever and ever!"

Revelation 5:13 (NIV)

May Your Praise Rise

Worship your Father in Spirit and in Truth.
There you will find ways of warfare praise.

Up out of the ashes and into the presence
of the Most High God.

Your praises declare His glory as you
put your trust in His wondrous ways.

Our Father in Heaven will never fail you,
but will valiantly prevail you forward.

This earth is a launching pad for heaven, and we
were not made for this world but rather for an
eternal reunion with our Father.

May His peace push us into praise,
and thankfulness in His love
make a way for miracles.

Our Father provides all that we need.
Take heart. He has overcome the world.

JASPERED JUNCTIONS

Jaspered junctions

Dazzling with love and light,

Twinkling your eyes with beaming joy

Illuminated awakenings

Droughts deemed for purposes

Parched longings satisfied and soothed

Harbored pain released

Feet unshackled

Captivity in the past

Justice junctions released for the weak and the wounded

For the modern-day Jobs, the jackal is silenced

Beaming rays of hope encompass the heroic mountains of His presence

Prospered peace is feeding my soul with sanctifying power,

Redeeming what has been lingering and lost

Function forward in the armor of Him

Arrayed in excellence

Equipped in love

Hope abounding, healing transpiring, grace unrelenting

Grace-gravity pulling me into the heart
of His healing haven and home of delight

The abandoned return home

Here and now, there are eclipsed entryways
and access points into the junctions of Jesus

You did not choose me, but I chose you and appointed you so that you might go and bear fruit—fruit that will last—and so that whatever you ask in my name the Father will give you.

JOHN 15:16 (NIV)

A Parting Blessing

Launch into your God-given destiny. Hear your assignment and act swiftly to obey your eternal Maker.

God has knit you together in your mother's womb before time in order that He should be known to all nations.

He has bound up your wounds and healed your every inner ache with the breath of His wind.

He has anointed and appointed you to bring good news to the captives.

He is seated on the throne of everlasting and is cheering you on in the heavenlies to finish as a good and faithful servant.

Those He chooses, He calls, and those He loves, He sends to bear upon your lives the testimony of Jesus' payment for sin.

Your sins have been canceled by and through the blood of the Lamb. Jesus has made a way for you to be face to face with your Father.

He is pleased with your willingness to obey, serve and follow Him no matter the cost.

The Lord rewards those who seek Him and those who leave it all behind to glorify His name.

Your Father in Heaven is proud of you.

Our Creative Team

Carrie Christopher
CoFounder | lionheartministry.com

Lynne Hudson
Illustrator | lynnehudson.com

Emily Walker Hall
Graphic Designer | emilywalkercreative.com

Lindsey Sullivan
Songwriter & Copyeditor | alabasterheart.co

www.ingramcontent.com/pod-product-compliance
Lightning Source LLC
Chambersburg PA
CBRC091203010526
44107CB00020B/1231